Vanished

Vanished

Poems by

Carolyn Beard Whitlow

Lotus Press
Detroit

First Edition

International Standard Book Number 0-916418-96-0
Library of Congress Control Number 2005933758

Printed and manufactured in the United States of America

This publisher is a proud member of

[clmp]

COUNCIL OF LITERARY MAGAZINES & PRESSES
w w w . c l m p . o r g

Lotus Press, Inc.
"Flower of a New Nile"
Post Office Box 21607
Detroit, Michigan 48221
www.lotuspress.org

Acknowledgments

Grateful acknowledgment is made to the following journals
where these poems first appeared:

"Baptismal" and *from* "Sorrow Songs" in *African American Review;*
"Black, I" and "On Charlevoix, Detroit, 1961" in *Callaloo;* "Grand-
father," in *Cold Mountain Review;* "Water Song," "Mercurial," "Still
Life," and "Basement" in *Crab Orchard Review;* "Soap Opera" in
Crone Chronicles: A Journal of Conscious Aging; "Home Schooled"
in *Dos Passos Review;* "Four Patch" in *5 A.M.;* "Herndon's" and
"Three Cent Stamp" in *Indiana Review;* "The Hour of Blue," "Book of
Ruth," "Local Call," and "Verily, Vérité" in *The Kenyon Review;*
"Pickpocket," "Positions," "Fugue," and "Wheatstraws" in *Many
Mountains Moving;* "African Basenji" and "Old School" in *Mochilla
Review;* "Space" in *Mockingbird;* "Boston T and Symphony" published
under the title "Three Songs for the Boston Subway" in *Mt. Olive
Review;* "Choo-Choo" and "Tortoise" in *Obsidian II;* "Brick House"
and "Sinkin'" in *Obsidian III;* "Husband" in *Tar Wolf Review;* and
"Vanished," "Chamois," and "Time and Money" published in a dif-
ferent version with the title "Over" in *13th Moon.*

"Beckoning" first appeared in the anthology, *Touched by Eros,* edited
and with an introduction by George Held (Islip: Live Poets Society,
2002). "Travel Paradelle" first appeared in *The Paradelle: An Antholo-
gy,* edited by Theresa M. Welford (Granada Hills: Red Hen Press,
2005).

This project is supported in part by an Artist's Project Grant from the
Rhode Island State Council on the Arts. The poet is extremely grateful
for having been named a Cave Canem Fellow and for two writing
residencies awarded by the Corporation of Yaddo which created time
and space to complete the manuscript.

Particular thanks to Molly Peacock, Marilyn Krysl, Marilyn Hacker,
Marilyn Nelson, Annie Finch, and Michael S. Harper for their
graciousness, encouragement and support.

For Joy and Abby,
ever and all ways—

and to the memory of my beloved brother,
Charles Julian Beard, II

Contents

AIN'T NOBODY HOME

Mercurial

Weight-lifted from a dream,
in the morning still
only a distant highway hum.
Get up! It's time for life.
Breakfast on eggs and little phallics,
sipping a pot of black,
words tumble from my lips,
communion toast, daily bread daily
prayer beaming balanced on my tongue—
poem on the Ford assembly line,
squeamish drivers, medicated functional,
traffic wheezing, congested,
clunker verb clogging the fast lane,
rear ends dovetailed, suspension low,
trucks butted over, horned,
parking spaces swallowed whole,
the lane dance of manners, etiquette
out of step, life, as in a movie,
punctuated with music, rap, club,
house, hip-hopped on the radio,
the press of stupid questions
literally making news, senators, old men
in robes, dowagers with lowered eyes
arguing over empires, history
rewritten on the American blank page,
streets illumined with electric sons,
Hermes glinting on the Mercurochrome hood,
and I blind, blinded, blindly follow.

Verily, Vérité

Classical minus Jazz? —the Blues—

I
On Screen

". . . you don't b'lieve I'm leavin'
try to catch the train I'm on . . ."

Blueblack hair slicked back
hot comb smooth, slimmer
not slender, trunk packed,
healthy, say she flat
chested a lie, sweet somethin'
a man wont to get a holt of,
squeeze some'nat natchal sugar, make juice,
thick nose spread to fine, sequin shimmers
stacked down to the nines,
stilettos tremblin', toes
tappin', her laugh like hand clappin', fingers
diamond ringed, eyes Rhine stoned, lashes low,
baubles lobed, spangles danglin', ruby
lipped slivers aquiver, two
teeth glinted gold behind'nat smile,
smoky spotlight pooled on a too small
stage, satin doll stylin' on the B-side,
hands hipped, beltin' out I pity
the fool leavin' south on the next train
goin' down, goin' slow slow down—
say she cry, cry, cry,

say love me, love me, say you do,
say love'll make you walk away,
lay love aside, walk away, she worry,
she worry the line, hum, scat, moan,
trumpet mumblin', backup whinin',
tenor guitar twangin'nem
 blues, strummin'nem blues, lyin',
tryin', cryin' blues, drumbeat foot stomp,
bass taut, microphone she hold like
a telephone to her heart, say,
"I gotta sang my song . . . "
"Say, you don't b'lieve I'm leavin'
         just watch the train I'm on . . .
Blink two times, Baby, blink twice,
Look up and I'll be gone . . .
Look up and I'll be gone . . . "

II
In Writing

Late. Awake. I enter into my journal:
"Illegible, now, the street sighs
on unintelligible streets, thickly settled,
the primacy the privacy of trees, green
with envy, waiting their turn. The story
again. And again. The minute, the moment,
the aftermoment, traveling, traveling still
in a place to grow older, old, no
digressions enjambed between the period

5

and capital; each minute distance, space,
the emotional void untended, inured, distance
hauled in, the point made larger, near.
A shallow in the water. A sliver of moon
on a plate of sky, forks of light darkening
cloud one lonesome sometime night. The luminous
heart of the digital ticks in syncopated meditation.

"A peddler of odds, ends of old intimacies
rattles door to door down rows of row houses,
train not fast enough or far. Neighbors
curtain their eyes, dawdle their meals, weariness
smudged into bones, return to the temperature
of war, biting sarcasm, wincing humor, grating
sounds of winey voices, the manicured among
the unwashed. Radiators cough up heat phlegms
of steam. Ice clinks against clenched teeth.
Visitors diddle dust bolls, long to rifle
the trash, pedestrians who never look back.
Every house, the night no different.
On TV a blue-lit club scene, blues singer . . . "

III
From Music

Clean unfolded sheets spread sound on the bed,
chords of color, pallet of blues, the squeaks
and moans of your jazz saxophone—"Alone

at Princeton Junction," "Monk Begging Alms,"
a thousand million angels take a leak in the sky,
dead bee on a wire scream, the let-me-go cry
of a tree-tied dog, spring mourning winter,
"West of Nowhere," "Hush, Now, Don't Explain"—
one line mumbled repeatedly but the whole song
left unsung. Scratch towel stiff from the line,
crisp but not mean, sloe-shouldered, you're
not a wing-tip type. Between the catch
of clutch and accelerator, the backward
roll, air pressure, blood. We are one.
We speak with one tongue. You cut my throat,
I sever your hand, the most pious the ones
who sin. Whole truths and half lies,
nothing else to offer, nothing left to take.
Neighbors bang a chorus of good-byes.

IV

The night swelters. I wash my body
of yours, mud pots and pumice, hug
the pillow for warmth. My dreams keep
me awake. "Good morning, Heartache,"
"the blues are brewin'." I sugar
my coffee cup, coffee with honey
and cream, long for something
sweet, the touch of your voice on my lips.
You're gone. Now words come like passion.
"I loves you . . . handle me with your hot . . . ."

By midnight know
The mailman won't deliver.

(By midnight know
The mailman won't deliver.)

I pull my own rotted teeth, keen the loss
of your sweetness. The dictionary screams
its words. I slam shut vowel-rot ears.

By midnight know
The mailman ain't gon' come.

(By midnight know
That male man ain't gon' come.)

V

The spiral stare of empty pages.
Pebbles of history pelting my brain,
lyrics dribble my chin, dangle
in my mother's voice, a tongue-tied gift.
The whang of white-boy guitar,
blue gums and stubble, fingers
with bar rot, playing on my heartbeat
a hamstrung, one string blues—

"Woke up this mornin', heard knockin',
    Sun beat down my windowpane.
Woke up this mornin', heard knockin',

8

Sun beat down my windowpane.
Wind whipped in whistlin', Lawd a Mercy,
Train tracks streaked my face like rain . . . . "

". . . Now lookee yonder, Sugar, where the
rising sun done gone.
Now lookee yonder, Sugar, where the
rising sun done gone.
I believe I will leave here Mama
a long way from my home. . . ."

Train tracks streaked my face like rain . . . .

Travel Paradelle

I travel through books, afraid to go outside.
I travel through books, afraid to go outside
where high strung telephone wires wind east.
Where high strung telephone wires wind east
through travel books, east to where strung high wires
wind, I go telephone outside, afraid—

a sightless pilot cited for steering blindly.
A sightless pilot cited for steering blindly,
plane bumps down, slides, slipping forward fast.
Plane bumps down, slides, slipping forward fast,
slipping down fast, forward, a plane slides,
pilot, sightless, cited for steering bumps blindly.

Woman orbits man; in stasis, he has the control.
Woman orbits man; in stasis, he has the control:
he's a train in her tunnel leaving no tracks.
He's a train in her tunnel leaving no tracks.
Woman has the control? A train man in stasis in her
tunnel? He orbits, leaving. No tracks! He's . . .

man, he's a train, fast, he slides where a pilot
has telephone control, bumps down blindly in her
wind tunnel leaving no tracks, plane in stasis
orbits the woman, cited for steering sightless,
high, east, through strung wires slipping forward.
Afraid to go where? Outside. I travel through books.

Giving

Pain comes in many colors,
this morning's green as blouse silk,
blush as my cheek brushed by your lips,
red as my unkissed smile.
I'm blue.
I see in your dark eyes that my night words
bruised your heart, you who teach
by example: love the man, not the look,
the person, not the image—
an apple no sweeter than its core.

So much of the world is superficial, synthetic,
illusionary—in this midst there is you,
honest, gentle, human, whole—
and I, mother of two, still forget
we enter this world sans silk or flax,
no gold nor green, but with a mind,
a voice, a heart, smile, cry,
the essentials if one has an eye for detail—
and yet I judge merit by the cut
of cloth, nails, hair, see frayed cuffs
and miss the textured fabric of your touch.
I cannot see my way to say good-bye.

The plane backs from the gate, underbelly
stuttered with suitcases of briefs,
deposed briefs in briefcases,

memories casualties of war.
The stewardess's plastic smile, uplifted
eyebrows lift me, my thoughts already airborne.
One eye closed, one blind, hearing blocked,
developed from a negative secondhand,
I sense you as though I'm flawless,
picture your presence as I imagine you to be,
more manicured, mannequin, bejeweled even,
undazzled by your diamond mind.

Radar on, course set, seat belt fast,
I ride as though I have no choices,
aisle seat, rows, each passenger in place,
straight-laced vodka man stage right,
beer king barreled on my left,
crushed linen look across, her creased-
pant lining hanging, *Good Housekeeping's*
"30 All-New Thirty Minute Recipes"
nested on her lap, sleepwalkers, all, napping.

Captive in this space, time, I watch clouds
accumulate, flocculus, look for a window
washer, imagine Patti La Belle warbling
a Judy Garland tune & flying geese
patterns, tremble with trebled breathing,
remember I tucked money in the book
you gave me and hid it on the shelf—
Is it the value of the words, or do you hold
my worth between the pages of your mind?

—contemplate angles, elbows, knees,
question neither gauge nor dash, nor landing
gears, question whether this journey is
my destination, rising up, going on,
giving in to getting off alone.

Tortoise

"Chug-chug, toot-toot,
off we go . . . "

I

Stumble-footed in tired attire, cara-
paced, bumped by the suitcase of the fumbler

in the aisle of the overcrowded Virginian,
she overhears the *cloche* hat ahead:

". . . don't have to take this shit to New York . . . ."
The smell of cigarettes slams shut.

Harried, she folds next to the attractive man
across from the unrhymed couplet,

sly with want to speak, to talk,
the race not to the swift but the victor.

He pretends not to watch her
read, write poetry, while he reads a novel

—the title of which she cannot see—
Abruptly he closes, perhaps to mull

and muse in lull of day while the train
treks south to the stars. With different

14

color stubs pinched overhead, they travel
together, alone, no hand held, no armrest

nor reststop between. Does he secret
what she writes, long to whisper truth? She

reads "Human Wishes" in *Human Wishes,*
longs only to be human. He

punches now, his calculator, a distraction,
a toy, a noise, jots hieroglyphic notes

of music or mathsuch, unfathomable, indecipherable,
damn near invisible through her no contact lenses,

his watch in blackface, grinning, tick-tock
of routine; she notes the automatic door—21122—stuck

II

Bangs and bangs 'til someone puts it out
of its misery. A woman at the spigot, water

trickles down her throat, neckline
plunged with a hammer, her ass genuflected,

brittle in the reflection of glass,
stares her downfall. A kaleidoscope

of trackside scenes snatches by, huffing and winded—
Blondie's Treehouse of Interior Horticulture,

The Food Emporium, NICE JEWISH BOY
MOVING AND STORAGE—1-800-NICE BOY—

pockets of men skirting the issues,
old men in cahoots with death, faded

paint signs on the crumble of brick,
filth and mud of human graffiti, contra-

dictions and indications, Broadway billboards,
nodders bobbing, chimneys, pipestems and steeples

of smoke, choked trafficways, bypassed
arteries, Christmas cameo church appearances,

metro commuters briefcased, platformed,
headed uptown with argyle smiles, *Glamour*

length nails, boarder guards armed at New Haven.
Inside, stenciled signs walled for the illiterate: —

DANGER: DO NOT TOUCH: EMERGENCY BRAKE:
FIRE EXTINGUISHER: NO

III

SMOKING. She's not hungry, at least for food, stomach
aches for love. Her seat companion hides his ring

hand. Naked is the other, and brown.
The girl behind asks a girlfriend,

"Are your parents still in love?"
Ravenous now, she munches, the bag empty

except for wind, unstops a cork of wine.
Three rows back a kerchiefed old Black woman

mourns spirituals, low, generations of pain,
recrosses Jerusalem next to the college boy

Jew. Back in the snack car, sardined men packed
in loud voices, corduroy champions of fifty

mouth one-words . . . "Hell". . . "Bill." Rock
slabs and towns slide by; two-bits of a mile

up a backside road the highway reek of carnage,
police uniform in uniforms, lawyer-chased

ambulance basted in blood. She remembers
she told her students a run-on sentence is like

the Amtrak and commuter rail that collided
then corroded in Boston, between them

17

a simple comma, the majestic semi-
colon dead. The hurt hadn't worn seatbelts.

Head crowded, she's in the waiting
room for life to begin soon, soon, everyone

with baggage. Stuffed full, the train gasps, farts.
Passengers belch out at Penn Station. "Excuse me,"

Brown Bread says, rising, coat shouldered,
hat cupped in hand. The train slakes on.

Day sips down to coffee, grinds to a halt.
Before bed, she smooths her arms, legs, flexed

feet with *Crema de Aceite de Tortuga*, yawns,
stretches, Pond's her face, unzips her shell.

Boston T and Symphony

I

Red Line

string musicians horn
for space underground, money
less than a token.

silently, silent
spirits of the living dead
ferry 'cross the Charles.

II

Green Line

loiterers jostle
stares; fat-narrow hips spread news-
papers, bags; tabloid

sideliners' headline:
"Shit Happens!" movers shaken:
lepers, Brahmins, Broughams.

advertisers hold
sway; silvered ringlets, gold hoops
dangle from stirrups;

left-wing students righted,
passengers in slow motion,
sneakers, loafers, heels.

feet shuffle along
anonymously familiar;
cookies tossed, coins, gun.

III
Blues

babe in arms the badge
that someone paid attention,
women-girls snap gum.

Choo-Choo

Chugalugga, Chugalugga, choo-choo train
Fast going nowhere, catch up runnin' behind—
My mind partly cloudy, tears fall like rain,
For the last, I mean the last, first time.

Going nowhere, fast, catch up running, behind,
I ain't ask that you forgive just understand
For the first, I mean the last, first, time
You my *Cane*, Daddy, you my sweetie, Sweet Man.

I ain't ask that you forgive just understand I didn't mean
        to — Hush! — do you no wrong;
You my Sugar Daddy, you my double sweet man.
Jus' I'ma young woman's old, he a young man strong.

Girl, I done ate beyond hunger, pleasure gone,
My mind partly cloudy, tear falls, rain,
So I'ma catch what's smokin', struttin' my song
Chugalugga, Chugalugga, choo-choo train.

—*for Herman Beavers*

21

rorschach

waters where I wade, recurrent—
ripples surface, nestle near shore.
on the hill a woman's house.
clean curtains breeze the wind—
kettle whistles a morning air.

plaited trees part the yard—
a garden sparrow scratches vainly,
gnats dancing about its head.

the path falls toward water,
laked, a duck dawdles among weeds.
as far as the eye can, sea vista—
shimmering eel-backed waves.

imagination warped, shore lapses.
my breasts reach for your hands.
words disjointed from my conscience crumble,
marrow squeezed from ashen bones.

my wings sail a heaven splattered starscape,
gliding I kiss a windstarved bird,
flit, silverscaled, through yellow-lighted kapok leaves,
crawl inside a water-logged twig that bites.

a snake rattling feathers rises
a sink hole plunges down the mouth of a jaguar

22

magpie howls choke macaques caw
egret udders flap across the cays.

border guards near mecca rake for contraband.
my fingers bracken, mottled in blood
sausage; dung beetle mounds,
rain coated, scuttle molten.

ink blots:
a city of cloud crags harbor a sky sea,
flight on the tip of my tongue.

BRICK HOUSE

Brick House

". . . a brick house,
she's mighty, mighty . . . ."
—The Commodores

I make no claims to the universe—

I own not even this space,
This skeleton of wood and brick,
But its heart pulse—mine—
Womb-warm rooms
Stretch marks of books lined against
Paint-skinned walls
Blemishes of art gilded and framed
Its rugs' napped, woven hair
Head flushed, body eclectic,
Vain with long-necked lamps
Flat-stomached tables
A muscular sink, sinewy stove

—Butt palmed in a sweaty armchair—
I chew glass, crush mortar, spit stones.

Cedar Closet

from "Sorrow Songs"

I. *Portrait in Baptist Pose*

> *"I told Jesus it would be all right*
> *if He changed my name . . .*
>
> *and He told me that I would go hungry*
> *if He changed my name."*

Jolly, Charlie Beard, church deacon, Mason,
fastidious in British plumes and sword,
gracefully paraded Atlanta Sundays
on the soles of his small dark feet,
shiny leather high tops buckled and laced.
Loved toffee, butterscotch and crème,
married a sweet chiffon confection,
peachy young daughter of Georgia teachers,
for her charm, grace and affection;
she liked to sit the porch and read
Romance books & church mags every week.
Charlie schooled to 4th grade, she commenced
8th, both born in the good-bad times
after the State of Georgia Reconstruction,
him in 1886, her in 1891.

How she ironed his shirt defines love.
Sunny Sadie Mae sewed and cooked, ribboned
hats to fancy, kept the house spit polish clean,
stretched window curtains, 35 cents each,
good pocket money in a week

to count dollar coins to seventeen
for laundry work and such.
All day wash, all day iron,
wash day Monday, Tuesday iron.
So proud was she of her name, home, man,
she wanted to do more and said,
"I don't have enough hands."

***

Charlie adored but left his mama,
a half-Negro gemstone Georgia Cherokee
full-blooded bodied woman, whose
given name was love. Harriet Love Beard.
Charlie's anthracite father, a merchant
who carted coal and wood by mule,
wakened Charlie many a child night
to sit by him in patched pants on the seat,
haul and hawk tired bags and corded bundles.
Charlie Beard eyed the sky each dawn
and with sure hand scissored the cotton clouds,
a fine white-coated barber he'd become,
clientele élite, the bone-white china men in town.

Sadie at sixteen could fish a good catch,
figured her dreams in the wish book
could come true; wanted to marry
so she could have a right nice family,
bore six of her own, two lived, one boy—
daughter graduated college, son high school.

30

"Ask anyone about their stock:
two shelves of canned goods over the sink,
one back behind the stove,
butter beans and string, ham and hominy,
potato pie too rich, too sweet to eat,"
no mention of Depression.
I know this to be true.
Sadie's last child, James, my father,
told my daughter Abby so.

Fish sold by pound, weighed by word,
and good's not always pretty.

II. *Sister*

"Sometimes I feel like a motherless chile . . ."

Mamie Lee could sit on her hair,
wore frilly frocks with flounces and pelisses,
pinafores, a size 3 shoe,
slept in a truckle bed.
Of an evening in dead time,
tree swing or porch glider
to sip the evening's cool,
a breathless need for air.
High strung, high yellow,
wouldn't eat no black folks' food.

31

Skin flushed, so sticky hot that night,
she dabbed and lightly fanned
a scented hankie, sky so clear
the cloudless stars seemed cold.
White suit slow-strolled the porch front by,
turned again and spoke.
"Evenin' back atcha," lowering her eyes.
She didn't mean to flirt
but, so young, giggled, tickled.
Rode shoe-fly from Savannah to Augusta,
ground divided not the sky,
boarded house on tenant ground.
Baby's uncle raised her.

***

Women of the church, they called Sister,
     Sister Reed   Sis Jones   Sister O'Dell

Sadie Mae called Mamie Lee Sister.
Say Mamie Lee *insisted*
Sadie Mae call her Sister.
Sister be too young be called MamaMotherMom.
Never cradled or cuddled, nudged or tucked,
never blew smoke in, to soothe her baby's ear,
furrowed fields turned to barley and wheat.

***

Bessie say she stayed with Sadie some
in Atlanta 'til '31—Bessie Swans,
Sadie Mae's first cousin.
Say, "Sadie had to walk far so far see Sister
'fore she died in the crazy house in Augusta."
She say, "Mamie Lee had Jim Crowed on the Atchison
up on to Chicago, and she and Marie Barnes
owned Club de Lisa there but Marie
Barnes stole her house and prop'ty
takin' care of Mamie's business."
She'd penny paid her $800 life insurance
policy but debts all that was left in the estate.
Mamie's second husband, Rev'ren Davis
molasses dark and sweet,
but she cottoned to high yellow,
upped and married Mr. Murray,
a Indian farmer what had billy goats,
cows and clabber, plums and peaches.
Some time back Mamie finished college,
Paine, in Augusta, taught there too.
And the Douglas Restaurant sat down
the street from Mamie's House of Beauty
what had plenty bidness, don'cha know.

Cousin Bessie say, "Bessie (Smith)
sho' could tear a tune to tatters." She hum herself
a little'n sang a bit'a 'Young Woman's Blues'—
"'I'm a good woman, I can get plenty mens . . . .'"
Then say, "Sadie wadn't much on church

33

but didn't allow no devil in,
called the stream ran by her house baptismal.
Her neighbors names? —now let me see,
Oh yeah, Miz Taylor and Miz Moon.
Yeah, Mamie Lee was downright pretty—
died Mamie Lee Fields Swans Davis Murray."

***

Mamie Lee, she born a Fields.
Family had prop'ty in Millen and Macon
and a piano in the parlor. Mamie Lee
claimed her people was always free,
they kin never worked no fields.
Now, that might could be a story but
Fields folks colorstruck for sure,
them Fields married dicty, Swans'n'em and such.
Mamie Fields' first husband tall
straight hair good looking
light-skinned teacher man wore a tie.
Swans flew by name of John.
Never, not known ever to had less than
500 worth of dollars in his pocket,
found roadside in a ditch, stone dead.
Some say John Swans Sadie's daddy,
others say they know better.
John Swans plucked bass guitar pizzicato,
his muscles strenuous sinews of sound.

III. *What Nobody Else Don't Want Somebody Else Does*

John Swans' brother had a name'a Fair.
Fair Swans' father first name Man.

Man Swans had a son name John.
Man Swans' other son he name Man.

Man Swans might could had a son name Cut.
Fair Swans taught at Morris Brown.

Fair Swans' daughter go by name of Bessie,
(Called Cousin Bessie by Mamie Lee).

John Swans might'a had a outside child
But Sadie Mae Fields called John Swans "Daddy."

When John Swans died her uncle, Fair,
Raised poor little Sadie Mae up after.

Mamie Lee never had a son.
Sister never did call her daughter "Daughter."

# # #

Herndon's

Lon himself emerged
hair bootblack black slick
shoes on marble tiles,
from between leather
green twin rows of chairs
to escort kindly
the white gentleman
personal smiling
to his brass-trimmed throne,
chandeliers crystal,
bronze, electric, white
steel ceilings, gold-rimmed
mirrors where to check
the trim, hushed buzz of
power and money.
Twenty-three black-faced
white suits stood their chairs
perfectly, whisk broom,
comb, pomade, iced cream
shaves, clippers, six-foot
long tubs bubbled clean.
Mustache waxed, nails oiled,
stoic and solemn,
"Sir, I owns this place,"
was all he said. *"This
barber name Charlie
Beard."* Lon had formal

schooling one year learned
himself to read, write,
cipher, no five'll
get you seb'n here.
Alonzo Herndon,
66 Peachtree
Street, Atlanta, knew
Niagara, Du Bois,
died at sixty-
nine, a millionaire,
in '27,
heavily insured.

Three Cent Stamp

PS. I heard that Sister Hamm is married.

If I don't hear from you soon I am
Going to call you and have it charge
To you will that be O.K.

July 2, 1949

1

Dear James,
I hope you and your family are well
and happy. I have only had two
letters from you in three months
and then you did not say if you had
heard from me. The only thing I
know my mail dont come back but still
that dont mean you are getting it
because it could get lost or go
to the wrong place. Well I know
one thing if you are not hearing
from us you dont care else
you would call and ask why you cant
hear from us. A lady that use to live
here but live there now was here to see
me this week and she said her girls
often tell her I seen James to-day
but they dont ever make them selves
known to you. I hardly miss a week
hearing from you though some one else.

38

2

Will you please tell me if you ever
feel bad because you dont care for
your Sister and Mother like you should?
I feel so bad all the time because every
body know you ask me how you are
and say he sure is a fine young man
and he was always a nice boy never gave
you any trouble and would never hang
around places wasnt nice and how fine
looking nice and friendly you were.
Poor Mrs Ramsey spent the day with me
this week and she is still talking
about your pretty hands. Mrs Ramsey
looks very bad she is real small Willie
Mae worries her so I wrote you about
Mrs Peek passing she wasnt in bed sick
her baby boy came to see her from Detroit
got here on Wednesday and Mrs Peek passed
that Monday says she got up that morning
said she felt bad laid back down and died.

3

Well I would be so happy if you
and all your family could and wanted
to come down to see your only sister
and mother this summer you could come
in the car. Other people children comes

39

to see them and I sure wish mine wanted
to come see me you already have a key
and you sure would be welcome very
welcome any time I dont even have to know
you are coming just take things as you
find them and be happy to be welcome.

4

The lady what is here from Detroit
has been knowing me before you were born.
Once her husband taken sick stay sick
a long time and they didnt have anything.
I felt sorry for them and push you
in your buggy one Saturday after noon nearly
all over South Atlanta and got up $6.00
and this was big money then because every
thing was cheap and more food than I could
put in the buggy with you and they were so
happy and she were with a baby and could
not work she says she will always love me
because I gave her food when she didnt even
have bread to eat now she is doing fine
and has money in the bank so she says.

5

Well I am very sad to-day this time
last year I was getting ready for a big
dinner for your Daddy and one of his
friends that work at the shop. This

friend of your Daddy is an old man
and his wife is dead and every time
he would come to see your Daddy when
he had his operation he would give him
a dollar and when he would know any
of the other barbers were coming out
here he would send him a dollar when
your Daddy got able to go the Dr. office
and come back by the shop he would give
him a dollar so your Daddy told me this
week one year ago soon as I felt like it
to fix a nice dinner for this old man.

6

So I did not put it off I fixed it right a
way witch was the first Sunday in July
on the fourth your Daddy went to church
that morning and brought back a gal.
of ice cream I cooked two chickens,
rice, peas carrots made hot rolls
and peach pickles I use my very best
I had just for him and his company
had flowers in the center of the table
and when his guess got here I served
them high balls in the living room
and they had such a good time. After
dinner they went for a ride and your
Daddy taken the old man home.

7

If I had not fixed dinner when I did
I would not have had a chance because
the old man soon left for New York City
to see a Son he has living there and he
did not get back until after your Daddy
passed well on that Monday witch were
the 5th but every body was home because
the 4th came on Sunday last year. I made
Bar-B-Q witch was the best I ever made
in all my life even the bones was good
and every body that ate some said it
was so good and your Daddy sure did eat
and it didnt even make him feel bad I
made spagghti had water melon also
chicken and ice cream left from that
Sunday and we went to ride that after
noon. So I cant keep from thinking
and cant help from being very sad
and lonely. Just think he will soon
be gone one year but he was so happy
even over his operation. I miss him
walking around here so much I have been
staying here at night all alone and not a
a light in the house wishing I could see
him but I cant. Please say if you got
this letter. Love to all

Mama

Linen Closet

Legacy

Mother loved Bartlett & Anjou,
licorice, peanut brittle,
astringent lemons, emollient olive oil,
should my daughters ever want
her hibiscus to unfold—

Wrapped packages at John Wanamaker's
worshipped at St. Philip's
adored symphonies & Ellington jazz
Billy Eckstein croons
(wasn't much for blues)
& pictures though not Van Der Zee
prove her size 5 shoes
stomped at the Savoy
stood in line at the Apollo
truckled off to Washington, D.C.
in government employ—

Lindy Hopped to Detroit, slipped
& snagged a Georgia boy
then polished to a shine
for seventeen years
her wool-scraped coat
so her children would be
haves not have nots
& spoke only to curse
fuss or scold . . . .

Struck by the sparsity,
what little I know,
phone my mother's brother, ask
their grandfather's name—

> *". . . Moses, I think . . . same as my father.*
> *Sorry. Folks just didn't talk back then."*

Secrets the only legacy.
Silence their only story.
Questions a sin.

Vanished

To my mother,
Ethel Winifred Coveney Beard,
1915-1975

1.

Away from Crusoe's deadpan
on Calypso's carnival isle,
your father's sea-captain father's
wood ship rocked you to America's shore
for the Great War, your face grave,
its pitch set as you crossed
the amniotic ocean,
your mother wretched, steeled
in the hull, baggage in the hold,
this our middle passage.
You came first, your brother lingered
yet two years in the womb.

Flogged by trades, windward, leeward, gusting
to Ellis Island, his mates called him *Cap 'n,*
your bloody handsome mariney mulatto father,
Moses to his people across the water,
navigator of this new archipelago,
this same Moses, this Elijah, this Coveney,
keelson brought forth by his English father
to bear his father's name—
his mother keening, a loon lost at sea.

46

2.

Skin lush dark as African-earth,
her billow-skirt, tender arms
a haven, your mother, your own,
marooned now on Manhattan's shore,
left you an island
in the flu epidemic of 1918.
At three, in your small eyes
she must have vanished,
her name never whispered at prayers,
verboten to speak of the dead.

3.

Ghost like, almost white, Ruth had cared
for the children of the Jewish master
furrier for whom landlocked Moses worked,
smoothing ruffled fur and feathers.
Ruth came to care for you.
But there was talk. Your father
thirteen years her senior, her but sixteen
more years than you, your stepmother's—
        (He waited three years, now thirty-five,
        a widower with two children)
—seamstress hands could not sow your smile,
found boxed, no bow, a sepia tinged portrait
you'd posed, faded daguerreotype eyes hollow,
creased full lips narrow, packets of old negatives.
Ruth did not raise your mother from the dead.

Keelhauled on command, you learned to fear
touch, the *Cap'n* stern, loyal and proper
British, no patois he, this patriarch's
        (Had his father beat him as a boy?)
brusque touch taught you to withhold—
beauty your hand writing, hands that loved
the language of violins. Sonatas
and études shimmered, Ruth silent.

I was sixteen when you told me,
        amnesia lifted, trembling
        phantom dark tintype in my hand,
that my grandmother was dead,
not distant, not Ruth.

        Now NPR and I consider all things,
speak of symphonic estrangements
as you sit gilt-framed collecting dust
to dust on the table.
        That you named me Ruth, a sign of love?

4.

My brother and sister dressed your body
for burial in Detroit, shipped your coffin
in the hold on unfurled wings
to an Anglican New York church
as to the island home from where
your father and mother vanished.

        I was not on board.

48

Hospitalized, holding on, close
that once you'd said,
"You know I loved you,"
ravaged by waves of pneumonia,
eruptions of pain, capsized
by stroke, sinking, eleven
operations, adrift
remembering us identical
in our blue sailor dresses.

Mother, how could I know?
You vanished
before I was born—

>   . . . I, all my life
>   submerged,
>   treading, waves ever rolling,
>   rising—
>   one nostril above
>   water,
>   from below no
>   raft
>   in sight . . . .

>   *By what faith*
>   *can I believe*
>   *that you*
>   *were ever*
>   *here?*

Grandfather,

I treasure as memory you pressed in navy,
Chest inflated as though medalled,
The cannon of your voice booming,
"I am a citizen of the Queen."

Whatever that meant I wanted
That command of attention, the pomp
Of that circumstance, eyes flocked on me,
This tiny seed child no one could see.

Oh, to be a queen!

To crush loaves of breadfruit,
Make islands from crumbs
So my grandfather could peck
Cocoa palmed in my hand.

But I am only a fowl of his seed.

I fly back to Scarborough,
A grandmother now looking for birth marks,
Taxi my way to Pigeon Point,
Grasping for straws to spin into gold.

I did not know her wealth was uncommon.
That queens are not the stuff of fairy tales.
That her royal subjects were objects.
Though loyal.

Home Schooled

In my parents' archaeology, I shook, swept under,
shoveled, foraged, sifted, excavated

dressed cadavers who awakened to spar—
Daddy, whose skin glowed, red oak gold-edged copper,

ever ready with barbed wire, stick and flint;
Mama, smoldering monthly around each lava flow,

sand wet with coffee colored, plump,
incendiary, skin paper bag thin.

Daddy strutted from his bath, towel draped arm
or shoulder; Mama laced her flannel gown,

white buttons cinched, neckline choked.
We slept in shifts—three sets

of wide child eyes watched
ice burn stick to stone.

The Nightgown

Blush flannel with tiny bows
crimped like my mother's,
my gown's modesty folds,
whisper soft crush across my breasts,
thighs, breathy, hot.

I lift its floral pink, peek,
look for a head,
hole hiding tongue,

its hand all the while
caressing my crease.
I want it to stop,

ask it to please—

Hear my mother's voice scolding,
dare her to knife me.

Hand and mouth daggers
drive me down killingly.

Basement

Whether empty-handed or with bags, books,
at the side door always a decision—
up to paper thin or down to cinder block walls.

Gravity compels, hauls me down, back to where
ever the sun is stingy on porous surfaces.
Strangle the chain cord of a naked bulb.

Behind criss-crossed clotheslines hung
with hard dried shirts in the dank,
hear the foot-pedaled ironer churn, roll

its hissing steam on flat-pressed
shorts, table linens, unstained sheets,
grapple, strain binding, magnetic force,

tensile strength in her hands' firm hold
on the cloth. Once, barely eleven, I toppled
the stairs. My mother stood glaring down,

her only words that time, "You know you can
get pregnant." Her only words this,
"Don't be an open road split like thighs."

Old School

My mother's navy, white trimmed suit
clung to my body like a woman's
meant for business in my eleventh year.
The question is, what business did I have
in that suit? My mother asked such developed
questions & going 45 rpm I wished for a miracle,
Temptations, Impressions,
sweatin' to the Drifters' oldies,
sang along with Motown in the mirror,
mouth poked out to kiss the mike,
snapped precocious fingers to Marvin's
"Can I Get a Witness?" Smokey's
"My Smile Is Just a Frown (turned upside down),"
Billie's "Ain't Nobody's Bizness If I Do."

My mother's trim swimsuit, navy, white, fit
my body like a woman's 'cause our hip pocket
address sweat in Detroit's black bottom,
penned in by skirted issues and vested interests.
Cut on the bias, money wore pin stripes.
And good luck had me naked.
In that weather I didn't care whether
what I wore was what I owned and Mama let me.
Sing, "Now ain't that peculiar?—a peculiarity."

My mother's trim white and navy suit
hugged my body like a woman's, horizon

hips, breasts in mountain range, thin-roped waist.
Thrill seekers gathered, watched the waves
lick, sun tickle, fish bite, sand nibble
children at play. One bright man said,
"There go some cherries," like he was shopping
for fruit. Splashing in, out, I heard a dark
deep voice put out, "Now that's a piece a trim."
I knew I didn't know it all right then.
Another man just rubbing his rising rubber. . .
"Rubber Ducky You're the One . . ."

On Charlevoix: Detroit, 1961

Eyes straight ahead, her heels
Tapped, tapped, tapped
Down the sidewalk, everything
In control except her hips.

The white Deuce and a Quarter
Eased slowly to the curb,
Smooth ship on a silent sea.

"Hey, Momma," soft and sensual.
"Hey, Momma," a second time.

She neither winced nor quivered,
Missed not a tap or beat,
Glanced not in his direction nor smiled.

That ship sailed slowly forward,
Neither listed nor lolled.

"You know," he said lightly,
"Even a dog'll wag his tail."
A blush. A giggle.
"That's better," he said and floored.

Four Patch

1945.

Second World War—
a night of truce,
her womb houses a wound,
shrapnel from a time bomb.
Her husband walks to work
at Chevy, or was it Ford?—
penniless on the graveyard shift
emptied by soldiers.

Hemorrhaging after afterbirth,
as she rests her strength sieves,
sandbagged, a one-minute egg timer.
Unable to hold, nurse, change,
her husband pokes holes in her armor,
drills her on her ailments,
demotes her to infantry,
his manhood regimental, air-tight:
he'll marshal the toddler boy.

Genealogic skirmish in utero survived,
Baby Girl stares at her mother
with her blind eye, cries with her good.

Coda: 1949.

Hysterical from a backroom abortion
her husband never forgave,
then another baby (girl):
she cut the whole thing out.

1954.

Delicately faceted though certain
in your dainty hands, Mama, barbs
too slight to catch the sun's glint
—indiscernible—except
each night when I squeeze the cloth
that wipes clear my tears
red swirls to the bottom of the washbowl.

Mama, why are you always angry,
& why do you hide
behind newspapers & mags
& when I seek say go away
& read a book but the girls in the books
aren't colored like me, Mama,
& the girls in my school are white, too, Mama,
& the dark girls on my street say I'm an e-light, Mama,
& my little sister is too little, Mama,
& my only best friend brother is away, away, away, away,
& the man by the pool hall follows me
with his eyes & I get scared, Mama,
when I watch TV

Words screamed in dreams
evaporate.
Cool morning sun.

1963.

In white and black Kodak snaps
placed in a keepbook I see a child
I do not know doing what I never did
in vignettes impromptu or posed, matte
cut-outs on glossy 3 x 5 or 4 x 6 rectangles,
scrap children trapped at different stages
with angled features recognizable
as my own curl from black bound
reconstruction paper, palpable apparitions,
fleshless stick figures with flawless skin,
gray-area-me invisible
as hands holding
tethers to hang a marionette.

Daddy, who knew Mason & Dixon well,
forbade me to cross the line.

I went to camp
for the summer
Bryn Afon in Rhinelander, Wisc.
to board scrub menstrual panties,
hot press blouses, undies, shorts & skirts

for little white princesses
who taught me what my mother had failed:
how to be a proper colored woman.

2001.

If on bits of old childhood cloth
again I could revel in primary colors,
trace with one finger the bias
on geometric, floral or animal prints,
snip frayed edges and worn spots, unblock
and square recollections, cut bolts
of fabrications into confetti or ribbons
to toss at a parade, add sampler swatches,
magenta, ocher, mauve,
scissor, press, piece, baste and sew—
a pattern of remembrance, as in a quilt,
might emerge, hand stitches binding
touchable memories together from scraps
of my hurt and snippets of your pain, Mama,
made textural, a textile picture book story.
And if we found a bled spot on the cloth
I could ask you, *Mama, you knew I was hurt?*
and you would answer, *Like you were my blood,*
patchwork framed, bordered black on white.

Hope Chest

Wedding Night, September

Lobbied hotel space.
Pan to a room.
A bed.
A man.
A man sleeping.
A man sleeping off his wedding.
A man sleeping off his wedding vow, high.

Where is the woman?
You mean his wife?
You mean the bride?

Sober in a chair in the room.
Empty in a chair in the room
with bare walls in her head.
Hollow in a chair in the somber room,
fairy tale finale on the bare walls,
movie with the charm prince
who will whisk her in white
off to the pleasureland of happy endings.
The endless happy endings once upon a time.

Why is this her dream?

She has not heard a blues song,
she needs to hear a blues.
Some things old, nothing's new,
borrow something, something blue.

Husband

I slipped, my lips unzipped,

into my voice like a dress.
"Feisty," you'd snapped back.

That word I did not know
hit like a fist—

It sounded, though, like fyce,
a term my Georgia father'd growl
to mark a mongrel dog.

"Heel," you could've trumped.
Or with your finger, point.
I'd have slunk down the corner.
Licked my womb.

Better, why not
curb me with a kick.
Then I could howl,
your foot in my mouth.

African Basenji

African Basenji: a dog of a breed originally from Africa,
having a short, smooth coat, and characterized by the
absence of a bark. [Bantu]: a member of any of several tribes
of central or southern Africa; also a Niger-Congo language.

Always shy, kept close to home,
no house play with neighborhood kids. I taught
doll school, confided in my dog—sister
cut against the bias from the same cloth,
brother gone. Daddy hated weekend mornings
when his women, warmed in robes, came downstairs.
My soft frizz curled under a frilly nightcap,
he'd say, "Don't come down here
those rollers in your hair,
go back put on some clothes." No light
in his light eyes, his strands crimped silk,
skin Cherokee brown. Sometimes he'd ease up
behind me, run his fingers through
the 'kitchen' at the nape of my neck,
scrinch up his face & say,
"eeeeeeeeuuuuuuuuaaaaahhhggggg,"
as if the spirals there, so unlike his own
or my sister's, offended him—

Pressed hair, length between ear and shoulder,
could go back— new neighborhood beautician
every two weeks for my wash and curl
seemed always washed up or washed out—

Once, reaching deep into my reticence
I asked & the lady fixing my hair
like to uummph me into yesterday:
"Did you hear what she said?" (said to
the other stylist like I wasn't there)
"What styles are girls wearing this fall?"
—her repetition mocking taunting me—
me who hardly talked to anyone at all
outside my home trying so hard
to make talk small, & didn't know what to say
or what she meant when she said about me,
"Oh, she has *that* kind of hair."

After I married, found an upper West
Side boutique for a wash, cut and curl,
made a second appointment in two weeks,
—me who'd grown up on the lower East where
change came monthly, regular like monthlies—

This beautician talked to me
& I glowed as she pattered along
about bits of nothing, told her stories,
one about her African Basenji.
Enchanted someone was talking *to* not about me
in this beauty shop, I didn't feel out of place,
nothing required other than to listen
snip of scissors & voice soothing, lulling
like rain as she handled the business

making me beautiful & she twirled
the chair to see my image in the mirror:
she had cut off *all* my hair.

Her wig line had not been moving.
Priced the one I wore home, to sell.
Knew one when she saw one: a dog with no bark.

Hair Catechism

Promised—never again—

to perm, press, relax my hair,
untrusting of beauticians.
Style set my big curly 'fro

in 50 little pink rollers—
To make maintenance free,
sculpted it shorter . . . shorter,

contoured to my pretty head
like a man's. Daddy hated
cropped 'do's, but Delilah-like,

no one could ever take me
by scissored-Sampson surprise.
Lake trip. Husband's mother

draped me in heavy veils—might
sun-darken on the water
darker than her son—

Stood over me as I sat
on her family room sofa
& touched my natural hair—

"ooooooooooaaaaaaaaaaaaaa-
aaaaaaahhhhhh," she shrilled,
recoiled her questioning hand,

". . . never seen such crinkly hair!"
post-Reconstruction response
dicty as my father's,

a Southern bread gentle man.
I had to undo her hair
lessons after my daughters'

Native-Euro-Afro hair
spent some summer time with her—
Lay 4-year-old's good hands on

my head: "Is Mommy's hair bad?"
"No, Mommy, I love your hair.
It's soft like fuzzy wool."

Task to undo history
no harder than a lioness
teaching her cubs not to kill.

Hickey

At twenty-six, I figured out my parents
had sex. I'd intuited,
given an older brother & younger sister,
but did not know for sure. As a child
I'd opened the nightstand drawer,
squeezed the K-Y Jelly,
snooped the recesses of my father's chest
to find old coins, stamps, certificates,
a letter meaningless to me & no secret
exposé of how they felt or why
they never touched or talked.

We lived on Detroit's lower eastside
six blocks from weekend matinees at the Dawn
for a nickel or dime. Even when the cost
rocketed to 25 cents—always—movie money
& somehow never scolded if we stayed
after the second feature & the short & newsreel
to see the start of the evening show.
Errol Flynn's "Robin Hood" was my first fantasy
man (I've always had a thing for green)
& I remember Eartha Kitt's rendition of "Santa
Baby" & "The Perils of Pauline."

Once when I was about sixteen my father
found some love letters I'd received
& left outside in a box under a tree.

He delivered each one personally
over the next few weeks,
rang the doorbell & I'd come
downstairs unsuspectingly each time
& he'd tip his hat & say, "Special Delivery."

When the red & purple-blue hickey appeared
on my neck I answered his "What is *that?*"
instantly, explaining innocently
that my 5" dangling initial—R—necklace
from my boyfriend Ronnie Williams
must have rubbed my neck. I couldn't fathom
my father would know a hickey if it bit him.
I was twice a mother & near divorce
before it dawned: *He knew.*

Book of Ruth

Whither thou goest . . . .

I learn to live by guile, to do without love.
I'm not scared. I wait in the dark for you,
Sleeping to avoid death, tired of sleep.
  The withered dyed rug fades, dims, fades, recolors,
  Warp frayed, weft unraveled; as light looms dark,
I doubt I'm happy as can be in this house.

  Outside no one would guess inside this house
I learn to live by guise, disguise my pain. Love
Dinner served by pyre light, sit doused by dark,
  Cornered in my room, wait in the dark for you.
  The bureau melts to shadow; that unraveled, uncolors.
Sleep to avoid death, tired of sleep,

  I avoid the mirror, the lie of truth. You sleep
Downstairs, chin lobbed over, chair rocked, spilled, house
Distilled in techtonic dreams of technicolor,
  Mostly golf course green and Triumph blue. I love
  Earthpots, cattails, a fireplace, no reflection of you.
While you sleep, I sip steeped ceremonial teas, dark

  As coffee, your swirled wineglass breathing dark
Downstairs fumes in the living dead room. Sleep
Comes easy, comes easy. I'm not scared. For you

71

I curtsy before your mother, say I love this house.
I love this house, this room. I love this. I love.
The traffic light blinks black and white. No color.

Come Monday, I'll dustmop, repaper with multicolor
Prints, zigzag zebra stripe rooms, fuchsias, no dark
Blue or sober gray, none of the colors that you love.
Insomnia is sweet, I think, the once I cannot sleep:
I'm not scared. I'm not scared. This is my house.
Illumined by darkness, I watch my dark mirror you.

No. No silent hostage to the dark, I know you
Cast a giant shadow in a grim fairy tale, colors
Bloodlet, blueblack, spineless yellow trim this house;
Escaped maroon, I emerge from a chrysalined dark,
Succumb, mesmered under a light spring-fed sleep,
Nightmare over, giddy, without sleep, with love.

The colors of the room fade into dust, house now dark.
I'm not scared. I learn to live without you, with love,
To do without sleeping to avoid death, tired of sleep.

BLUE SKY

Space

This, a must write night,
thoughts sieve through my mind,
grit, sand, head split off
its hinges, swinging
like a broken door.
I pour one cup of words,
slosh vowels in my saucer,
slurp, frittered remembrances
timid with spice.
Depth sounding failed,
letters jostle, spill,
mumbled pick-up stix,
pretty little prints.
A silent taste in my mouth,
sentences beaux-tired,
merry gentlemen choruses
lip-sync Southern comfort,
joy, warble bassoons' bass
joviality, music unconscious,
inaudible, tinsel tinkling
ice. No screw driver handy,
pregnant with expectation,
like a Christmas package rum-
bled, dropped, oops, burps,
regurge, bursts, these lines break
open: red-eyed across tablecloth
rectangles, time squared,
I empty into space.

Baptismal

Run, Eliza . . . run from Simon . . . .

A slip of ice on the river—
Current running, falls,
Wounded rocks embedded,

Bruised rivermouth agape.
Bloodspools, strung waterbeads
Skirt spindle thighs.

Moiling—
Gloam of huddled light. Touchfires.
Wet breasts bound, anklegagged,
Whiskey-breath communion.

Broidered men in carpet slippers,
Noose-neck ties; ruffled
Staunch Sunday waists, the women,

Next of local kin; issues loom large
In the small hours of morning:
Windstripped, clothesline hung

Body dressed with two hundred stripes,
Fresh cuts in every room. Home.
Couch an overstuffed

Tattooed stomach, coat
Slouched back a chair,
Grim chin and jaw,

Holy bric-a-brac, doilies—
Daguerreotype memories saved
In tinny, gaseous air . . . .

Local Call

You handle me like I'm a local call.
I'm expensive. Long distance—although
having never been loved I don't know how

to tell you so. So I answer the phone,
anticipate its diamond ring and let
you handle me like I'm a local call,

your line old as an old simile, stale
as a dead metaphor, you who's always had,
having. Never been loved, I don't know how

not to wish you would not stop stop not
loving me, the sidewalk running past me,
you handle me like I'm a local, call,

laugh in another language, hung phone screaming,
me unsure whether my anger volcano or match—
I don't know, having never been loved, how

to love, my mind stalled with graffiti,
imagination sore, hum "Don't want nobody
don't want me," accept your local call,
having never been loved, knowing I don't know how.

Black, I

an old-movie buff—
an old, movie buff

Cauliflowered,
I stand in the kitchen—
Egg-planted,
Second banana to a buffoon.
My body's so love wounded
There's no where for words to cut.

My eye is swollen, closed.
I am entombed, silent as an old movie.
My words crowd, roped in,
Jeering prize fighter lips.

My lungs' bellow blows
Heart fire; this anvilled head rings,
And I've loved you since
The day I wore blue.

—for Toni Morrison

Chamois

rain trickles the leaves—
giggling,
all fall down . . .

Mop the ocean floor,
Water warmer than air,
Morning darker than night.
Broom in hand I dare to speak
But for my axen tongue.
Whisper, whisper at vespers, pray.

Mirrored windows polished, glimpses,
Old, of hands, pound
Cake fists, sugared veins
Granulated, clotted butter
Iced in winter rain.
Frowns come in waves, in waves, slap
Shored against a kiss, breasts powdered
With milk. Clean sweep. Clean

Sweep each corner, crevice, rootbound
Pot, socket, pore, tombed
Vestibule, parlor, sitting rooms,
Closed doors, basemented highboy, sideboard.
Fingers of trees grip the earth,
Spleen split at the root.
Vultures listen for predators, prey,
Talons laughing; teeth and tongue,
Chorded, strangle heart-warbled harmonies.

Oven off, pyre grey, the word, three
Thousand hundred voices, inflamed, palimpsest
Burned, evensong altar of innocence,
Honey, oil, sponge a twinge of vinegar,
Sweet pungent blood. Oh! the sash and swagger
As my quartered hinds kneel
Before you, my Agamemnon,
Emperor of my tiny space.

Time and Money

7:30 a.m. or $7.30, what matter?

I drop out of dream into day,
mind a muddle, imagination
submerged, shower startled
body gargled with soap,
tremble, water so cold
words rush in a vowelfall,
streams stingy with thought
fast down the drain.
Body parts oiled and working,
adorned to be adored,
you walled behind *The Wall
Street Journal* columns'
rise and fall over eggs
over easy, toast dry,
still I drink you in for breakfast
flavored with half a cup
of half and half and half
a cup of skim like that
will make me whole. Look,
if a double decimal
denotes the only difference
between time and money,
what is the point?
Cost benefit analysis says,
if for us a tree means green
backs to you and infinitives

like 'to leave' to me—
If energy invested is optimized
but there's no percentage yield,
no flex time, if why? questions
suggest 'ex' to the power of one,
the quotient must be a zero sum game
unless at half after seven this evening
I reset my morning clock for $7 mill,
then drop off the day into beauty sleep.
Or I could calculate a better use for my time.

Fugue

can see but not read
can read but not think
can think but not speak
the spoken unheard
the unheard written:

I scrub my hair with a floor brush,
dustmop my mouth, broomsweep my crotch,
womb inside a body pressed
to service like a dress worn thin—
sit by the window, naked
panes before me, write
archival footage, linger
over the page longingly, words
languid, grounded suspension of disbelief—
my ears stoop to listen,
emotions exposed like genitals
flashed, covered, flashed, neon
darkness, staccato light pulse
failed, envelope stuffed with male,
plain-cover rejections hand-stamped, post-
marked, my mind giftboxed, tongue-tied, bowed
under, avalanched, buried
by thoughts unasked, unowned, not my own,
here and there a button pressed,
thoughts contained, words out on parole,
distrust a trust I must keep—
l-e-t-t-e-r-w-o-r-d-s whisper, sibilant,
labial voices in fugue, fuse, ignite
the darkening bloused within me
and I behind the blind do see

84

the difference between the poems
that live, those lines that
survive, these letters hung
on the lifeline
d(r)ying.

Wheatstraws

As night, each night, stays day—
I turn the corner of consciousness, near
morning. Beside the bed a cordial

of crystal, a half-carafe
of now vintage sweet. I feel you
so acutely still, hold you

in contempt, roll over
like a cheap and skinny lay.
Staggering from hands

where tongue and teeth can't go,
I genuflect over the font,
bladder-mixed wine and water,

too flush with words to speak.
The paste of jarred bowels.
The sink of cold air.

A man you tell by his woman,
a woman by her pots.
Each scoured month I dust,

throw out wads
of old blood, sweet
eating ants, my wounds

fresh as meat. Lovers
can lie. Friends must tell
truth: "Give me your pain,

I'll take it outside."
Clouds border a sky lake, blue
the color of distance.

Down hill, wheat
straws suck Earth.
I squeeze from my breasts

milk curdled, mush,
feed like Neruda's woman—
my hands strong, firm, whole, wheat.

Pickpocket

The Taj Mahal, our favorite restaurant,
has closed. You spirit all our old spots
which I revisit once and again, time
after time. I go in after the rush,
sit alone, gaze over the menu, order
my heart's content. There's no doubt
who will pick up the check. I eat
our pungent favorite dishes, raita,
masalas, dal, curry hot enough to cry.
Your eyes used to catch my words as they
tumbled from my tongue, our last supper
a vault of silence. I watched you
not watch me, concentrated on your chew
as though you were a dentist concerned
with bite. On today's menu, one from column
A, two from the column to be—I am, I am.

Women dining alone catch up on their mail,
read junk like stock reports, novels
peopled with people, eyes never rising
from plate or page. The waiters, their words
audible in a language I don't understand,
clink around me, setting up for those
they know will come. I squeeze shut
my legs and moan, the tabled flowers
artificial, linen cloth covered with glass,
emotions spilled mopped up easily

with the quicker picker upper.
The restaurant empties like a stomach,
a lone couple fused in one corner—
I wait for them to come out fighting.
As the sweaty cook steams from the kitchen,
my waiter bows, hands me a fortune cookie:
"Buy a man shoes and he will walk."
I pocket it, unpurse my lips and money,
wander the city, steeled, hoping to be picked.

Sinkin'

Moon shine in the sunshine
    don't shine much a'tall.

        Moonshine when the sun shine,
            don't shine much a'tall.

                Cock crow in the hen house—
                    sho' is a flo' show.

An' you a sweet som'in, Daddy,
    long as you is tall.

        Say, you a sweet som'in, Poppa,
            long as you is tall.

                But when I starts to lovin'
                    my windfall's a short fall.

Need more coffee in my coffee, Honey,
    don't want no sugar in my tea.

        Coffee black, Honey,
            don't want no sugar in my tea.

                Wanna feel, when you lovin' me, Daddy,
                    ocean drownin' in my sea.

Boat be rockin' even on dry land.
Say, I need my boat be rockin',
rockin' on dry land—

Current take me under,
Sun can't, moon can—

Ain't had no lover las' some years
'cept me.

Ain't had no lovin' last for years
'cept me—

Gon' find another lover,
snake, or rock or tree.

Sunshine sinkin' in moonshine
don't shine much a'tall.

Moonshine drownin' in sunshine,
don't shine much at all.

Cock, Crow, in the henhouse
sho' is a flo' show—

—*for Sherley Anne Williams, in memoriam*

Blue Sky

I hunker down among Maroons,
those encyclopedic regiments
bivouacked on the shelves,
one opened to M—Macéio, Madagascar,
Madrid, Martinique, matador—
lap cat blanketing my thighs,
her memories of heat radiating.
Still cold, I rise, bleed veins of silver:
the radiator hisses and growls.
Upstairs the bed too somber to slumber,
I imagine warm rooms peopled with love,
spartan furnishings, no trappings of gilt.

I long for my two daughters,
one fording a rivery rain forest, land
empoldered, yucca and succulents glutted,
gorged, huts struggling uphill, marginals
working class, intelligentsia élite—
Or she stands in urinated water writing
on stones stories lived but unwritten,
photographer of negatives, graven images,
myths of Christianity rampant,
wrestling childhood boas from 'round
her shoulders, innocence shed, green
leaf browning in the sun. She left me
Allende, *The House of the Spirits,*
took *Doña Flor.*

The other one nestled all snug,
tucked from bully boys with zippers
filled with snakes and no hero dad riding herd.
I crack open her door, handlamp piercing
the room with interrogation intensity.
Her even, vaporized breathing lulls me,
sleep rising like steam. She, too, knows
survival by a mere breath. But she trusts.
Windows at bay, I hide behind sheer ruffles,
peachy double-folded pleats. Outside,
silhouetted trees, snow-beaten earth.
The moon turns, faces me. Then, barely audible
above the radio whispered symphony,
her voice mumbles, "Mom, is that you?"
to this robber of piglet banks.
The river pours backward, stars retrace
their steps, meld with the sea-
merging shore.

I doctor some coffee, a pot-
boil of roots, *Cane,* sugar, return
to my rocker, me tottering at the edge—
Think cursorily about the former student
who called for the umpteenth recommendation,
this time her life, direction, in order.
I smile, remembering my "No," not dramatic
but assured. Sometimes language is so
simple: thunder stumbles, rain falls.
I sit a moment more, stroke

the striped, dotted tail
awash again across my lap.
Overheard, distant, a garbage truck's churn
signaling 5:00 a.m. Then resounding silence.
"Be bullish," I say. *"Think blue sky.*
One month more, light at this hour."

        As through the skylight peephole
moon and dawn caress,
darkly I climb the stairs.

The Hour of Blue

nickels of daylight spent,
night an empty pocket . . .

. . . caught between thought and sleep,
coffee pumping blood, veins, arteries
needled by handsewn sentences, mind
       stained paper, alphabet letters frenzied,
       no, ordered, glissandos colored crooked
       striped, all very one two three, by ear,
            not note, sentence in the word, in the word
            the meaning, mode, Church of God of Prophecy,
               circumference of continuity, hysteria
of complacency, declaration of blue jukebox
fugue thumped on tin pianos in one thousand-
ten towns, chords of words from seven notes,
       ear drum drummer tongue bursting the beat,
       split tympanum slurred electric trombone slide—
       sentence in the word, the word the meaning merged,
           paradox of complexity,
           the word spoken, buried, unearthed
       still the word, vowels handworked, creweled,
double-double *u*, conundrums drumming,
silent tongued shoes sloshing diphthongs,
dimple of an *s*, slick *c*, curved *r*, suspended
       animation: apostrophes overhovering a wobble
       of words, mélange, gumbo of sound, fingersnap,
       CLAP, jazz piano fingers, symphonic hands, clavicle,
           cello and oboe legato, key of G, C, A-

minor fugue in B-flat black-keyed cash:
$20 dinners, a raw taste in my mouth,
no currency (t)o (i)nsure (p)romptness,
no saddle of lamb, filet beef, veal mousse—
    dark light beer, ragtime piano rolls, slaw,
      red-eye on meat and potatoes, clotted throat
          scaling tuna from bones, insides gutless, gutted,
          Bonita and Albacore, Minerva and Waltham,
slow dance the waltz of the blues . . . two, three,
one, two, three-quarter two-step stop time, one
      blues' husky moan: "Bessie Mae, Bessie Mae Mucho . . ."
      (female fine-tuned bass player in an all male jazz band)
—eleven after thirty the hour of blue,
monochrome blue, mean blue, median, mode,
human woman's minstrel heart red-tired 'round midnight,
'round (SOME) midnight (DAY)
    nothing fair or sacred,
    'round midnight (MY) kind of blue, 'round
        midnight (PRINCE) 'round midnight (WILL)
      'round midnight (COME)
    'round midnight cheap talk ain't small:
    only punctuation holds my tongue.

Positions

1.

This is a day of impositions.

2.

Held now by chains of forgetfulness,
Unopened gates, the inner sanctum
Still, subliminal, labyrinthine,
My limber fingers tiptoe
Past Pandora's sealed box.

3.

Your back a blackboard,
Fingers of soap—
This is a day of impositions:
My inner sanctum still,
Your lips, hands,
My many mounds—
My mind enters my womb,
Dives down down
To the bottomfilled depth,
Subliminal, labyrinthine.

4.

Held now by chains of fullness,
This is a day of impositions.
You turn me
Like an egg over soft,

Beat my drum slowly,
Drum song dance
Tongue talking:
Tautness reverberates, cymbals resound,
Pandora's unsealed box.

5.

This is a day of positions.
I give you my body
—a gift—
Legs wrapped 'round your back
Like ribbons,
Feet tied in a bow.

6.

Pandora's sanctum unsealed,
Subliminal, labyrinthine,
Unstill, open—
My hips become peasant,
Calves and beeves,
My mind before me a melon,
Seed after seed after seed.

Soap Opera

Old age creeps up on me.
I hush its welcome, stifle
this newborn child.

Doubleblind. TV turned on
stereo loud, VCR finally tuned,
I mumble among collected books
as though to touch them
is to read, fingers
ever hungry, fingertips numb,
mind insatiable, weak,
stopped time clock watched
like a stovetop pot,
hope chest filled with sags of milk,
heart, big as my bed, empty.

Seeking the heal of words,
need for touch fire-light,
I sew my womb closed,
dust my clit, shudder
behind blinds and shutters,
cook my ovaries, serve them.
Dishes pretty the meal,
tomato wheels and avocado
moon on crock and ceramic,
halved lime boat afloat.
Food plumps my breasts like pillows:

Handsome, you enter my woods
lost in finding yourself,
waft in this softness—
my stomach rounds the bend,
butterthighs like surfaced cream,
ginger skin brown-baked
like bread. You pry, open
my lips, search with your
tongue for losses,
sip and blow the steam—
bodies ground to fine,
skins milked down smooth . . . .

. . . Disheveled, housecoat open,
I put down my glass of suds,
hear dishes crashed in the kitchen
sink, my mind on men—
a pause, then, hands wet,
feel Brailled in fine print
on the serial box:
some self-assembly required.

Water Song

Smooth FM 99.1—

. . . headache distant thunder tumbling   dry rain
thirsts on my cheeks   winded   rudderless   dream-
          starved   somnolent   to sleep a gift
mindwaves waft, humid   ice tinkles melt down to music,
          quarter notes and halves drip into song
     soda limed with "Amaretto," "Mountain Dance," water

rum soaked   Kilauea's lush mudslide   rocky whitewater-
fall   mind tumbled   static wedged between rain-
     drops   saxophone cloudy Gyra skyblued   club
     scene drenched, windy with song   I doze   dream
lighteningly fast, thunder limber   xylophones drum music,
     "Shaker Song" Spyroing   jazz cumulus   gift-

boxed horns swing out, sister   strummed ripples gifted,
double-bass almost vocal   cymbals hesitant   tempo at water
     temperature   hot   cool   anything but tepid music
          shaken hipswung tunes, timbrelous, rain-
down tremulous   arpeggios gurgle, submerge, drown   dream
     song resonant   thunderous   like roun' New Orleans clubs

memories soused on Bourbon   groove dubbed late, club
     nights in L.A.   some downhome blues chanteuse, gifted
     songstress   dress C#   key B-flat   her solo dream
     stagestuck   breathless   listeners   eyes water-
lily tender   mesmered from harmonies sprinkled with rain.
     Even the moon listens, shimmers with music—

chants   traditionals   funk   hymns   madrigals   musicals
blued by saxophone catarrh, oboe rounds, club-
set Bony, drum-men, Enya's "Caribbean Blue," her rain-
forest sounds trickled like rainsticks, suddenly her gift
sodden, cloud-rich, as when after moon rainwater
falls, eighth notes soak into mudthick whole dreams . . .

Ahh, Brook's tune "Rainy Night in Georgia . . . " dreamily
. . . Ummmmmm. . .
Tender Jarreau croons "Susan's Song," buttercream music
sweet spicysour like Thai Shrimp in Love on water-
cress, Seafood Typhoon, Mussels Yum-Yum, club-
footed lobster, Dancing Squid, all my birthday dishes, gifts
from laughing Susan,
fifty balloons somewhere over the rainbow,

each wish dreamed in amazing technicolor, friendlove gift-
wrapped 'round us, our beribboned streetsongs water
music, two raindrops harmonizing outside some Boston club . . . .

—for Susan Maze-Rothstein

102

Beckoning

I'd love to see you come to me again,
Come down, come 'round, come near,
While you, while away from me, think of me

Less, think of me not, think of me once
Maybe now and then, or twice a month, or year,
I'd love to see you. Come to me again

Before it's noon, or night, or cold,
By spring, at dawn, before you're old, for while
You wile time away, you could think of me

Lusciously reclined, liquid, quietly longing
Only for you, needing you to feel how much
I'd love to see you. Come to me, again,

Turn up, turn back, come on,
Come here, face my magnetic pull, drive in.
You know, while away from me you think of me,

And when you come, as I know you'll come,
Whisper, ask, and I will sigh deeply and say
I'd love to see you come again when you
Say to me you think of me while away from me.

I'd love—to see you come.

Still Life

Paintings alliterate this home,
each brush stoke full with music, words—

Gorman's Men of Taos brood,
Eng Tay's Two sit in walled refuge,

Richard Yarde's blues see Zora doubled,
crocuses tremble, elephant herd prints,

abstracts, lithographs,
triptych and oils collage,

cacophony, euphony, symphony.
Framed over the mantel

from their every angle a view,
sky at its hem fire-rose,

blush rising in waves over azure hues.
I step in, toes touch sand,

hold my own hand, meander alone.

This is still life.

Mantra in the Morning

I went away and met myself a new
brand, no one knew me, brand new me,
the time seven and change in the morning

for a change, no more tourist in your own life,
imposter wearing your body, living your life.
I went away and met my self, a new

self, woman with voice for a change, virtuoso,
voice its own instrument, arranger, conductor,
the time for change seven in the morning.

For a change go away, change if you want to,
just change anyway, any way you want to:
I went away, met myself anew, a new

brand, no one knew me, brand new me,
and you can, you can change this time,
the time seven and change in the morning

at seven, or seventy, change, seven come
eleven times seven, change brands, just change
at seven and change the time in the morning.
I went away and met my new self anew.

Notes

"Travel Paradelle": A paradelle is a contemporary repetitive poetic form designed by former United States Poet Laureate Billy Collins.

from "Sorrow Songs": Mamie Lee Fields was born *circa* 1875, probably in Tennessee. She attended and taught at Paine Institute in Augusta, Georgia, re-chartered as Paine College in 1903, at a time when there were no public schools for blacks, so Paine served as both a secondary school and a college.

"Herndon's": Freed slave Alonzo Herndon (1858-1927) was one of the first African American millionaires in the South. He owned Herndon's in Atlanta, located at 66 Peachtree Street, which catered to white patrons only and was known from Richmond to Mobile as the best barbershop in the South. Charlie Beard was a barber in that shop. Herndon, who had joined the Niagara Movement founded by W.E.B. Du Bois, acquired over one hundred residential houses as well as a large commercial block of properties. In 1905, he founded the Atlanta Life Insurance Company, the largest African American-owned business in the country.

"Three Cent Stamp": This found poem is an actual letter written by Atlanta resident Sadie Mae (Fields) Beard, Charlie Beard's wife, to their only son, James Fletcher Beard, then a resident of Detroit.

"Legacy": Ethel Winifred Coveney, a member of the United Office and Professional Workers of America, Local 16 in New York City, transferred to the United Federal Workers Union in October, 1942 and moved to Washington, D.C. By early 1943, she relocated to Detroit and six weeks after she met James Fletcher Beard, who had migrated from Atlanta, they became engaged on her birthday, April 15, 1943. They married at St. Cyprian's Episcopal Church in Detroit, Michigan on May 29, 1943.

"Vanished": Pregnant with her third child, dark-skinned Mildred (Williams) Coveney died of pneumonia in Harlem Hospital on October 15, 1918. Widower Moses Coveney, a mulatto, remarried on March 21, 1921 to Ruth Rebecca Butler, his fair-skinned babysitter, before the Manhattan city clerk. Documentation shows he visited Mildred Coveney's gravesite at St. Michael's Cemetery (Episcopal) in Astoria, Long Island on October 24, 1926.

"Four Patch":

1945: The Ford Motor Company assembly line had turned to the manufacture of small parts during World War II, which ended in August, 1945. During World War II, the branches of the Armed Forces were segregated. The speaker was born via Caesarian section on March 26, 1945; her brother, Charles J. Beard, II, was born December 24, 1943.

1954: The United States Supreme Court, in *Brown v. Board of Education of Topeka, Kansas,* ruled that segregation in public schools violated the Fourteenth Amendment. Lower courts were ordered to use "all deliberate speed" in admitting Negro children to public schools. The speaker attended integrated schools in Detroit, Michigan at the time.

1963: The violence that occurred in response to peaceful Civil Rights demonstrations across the South was televised in black and white. Crossing the Mason-Dixon line signified entering the segregated South.

About the Author

Selected as one of ten North Carolina poets to appear on the 1997 series, "Poetry Live," hosted by Charles Kuralt, recipient of a 2001 and 2002 Yaddo residency, and a Cave Canem fellow, Carolyn Beard Whitlow is a Charles A. Dana professor of English at Guilford College in Greensboro, North Carolina, where she teaches creative writing and African American literature. She was finalist for the 1991 Barnard New Women Poets Prize and the 2005 Ohio State University Poetry Prize. Professor Whitlow wrote her first poem at thirty years old while she was a Ph.D. candidate at Cornell University. Subsequently, she completed the M.F.A. degree at Brown University where she won the Rose Low Rome Memorial Prize in Poetry and was named Phi Beta Kappa Poet in 1989. Lost Roads published her first collection of poems, *Wild Meat*, in 1986. Her poems and essays have appeared in numerous journals and anthologies.